The Comical
Macker

Cormac G. McDermott BA MEconSc

Order this book online at www.trafford.com
or email orders@trafford.com

Most Trafford titles are also available at major online book retailers.

Printed in the United States of America.

ISBN: 978-1-4669-9001-2 (sc)
ISBN: 978-1-4669-9000-5 (e)

Trafford rev. 04/15/2013

 www.trafford.com

North America & international
toll-free: 1 888 232 4444 (USA & Canada)
phone: 250 383 6864 ♦ fax: 812 355 4082

CONTENTS

Chapter 1: Story Glory   1

Chapter 2: The Name Game   20

Chapter 3: Some Bloke for a Joke   24

Chapter 4: Stream of Consciousness   35

Chapter 5: It is I Who is the Greatest!   40

Chapter 6: A Book of Revelations   43

Chapter 7: Fond of a Double Entendre   55

Acknowledgements   63

CHAPTER 1

STORY GLORY

The lads I used to play football with on a local team decided they would have a re-union over-40's clash . . . . approaching kick-off time one of the sides only had ten players . . . . a guy who was on the sidelines wanted to take part for the under-strength team . . . . the only problem is that he had about six pints in a local boozer before going up to watch the game . . . . the lads came to the conclusion it wouldn't be a problem as it was not a serious match . . . . they told him he could play in goal and with two minutes to go the side he was on were winning four-nil . . . . however, he turned his back on the play to relieve himself and when he did the opposition broke up-field and scored in his unattended goal . . . . it brought a huge uproar of laughter from all who were playing in the fixture and on the sidelines . . . . I remarked that because he went for a piddle it destroyed his clean sheet and that this bloke should now be referred to as 'P*ssed His Bed' which everybody thought was funny . . . . the nickname has stuck with him and the story gets a good chuckle out of everyone whenever it is re-told!

I was looking at the menu from my local Chinese take away one night when I spotted an option called 'Yuk sung' . . . . I thought 'that sounds gross . . . . I mean, any dish that has 'Yuk' as part of its' name would be a real turn off for me and a lot of other people too I'd imagine'!

I was stopped by these tourists once in Temple Bar, Dublin who asked for directions to the Greek's Head Bar . . . . I replied 'No worries lads, just walk straight up until you come to a street called Parliament St . . . . now you will know this street if you look left and see the City Hall building with a big green top because it got licked like an ice cream by a female leprechaun' . . . . and to quote some other witty Dub 'The Greek's Head' is two and a half feet from his genitals'!

I entered a bar once and enquired if the vertically challenged manager would show the football while live music was on but was told 'No' because he was 'grumpy' . . . . I tried to cheer the man up by saying 'so you are Grumpy . . . . well, may I suggest that you not to be so Dopey and turn on the sport as Snow White and the rest of the dwarfs have given you the go-ahead to do so' . . . . it got me barred from the place!

I was in a bar in Dublin recently where it cost me EURO7 for a rock shandy . . . . I thought to myself that I could have got The Rock Of Gibraltar, the rest of Spain and all the cheeky purple-arsed baboon monkeys that roam the kip for less!

There was a guy I once knew who my pals told me had a very humorous habit . . . . they dared me into striking up a conversation with him to see if what people said about him was true . . . . here's a fictitious conversation between us one time!

ME: 'Hey mate, were you playing footie yesterday?'!
MATE: 'Aw yeah Macker, I saved two pennos and kept a clean
    sheet' . . . . he proceeds to tap his genitals twice!

ME: 'Hey mate, did you go out last night?'!
MATE: 'Aw yeah Macker, drank twelve pints and shagged two
    birds' . . . . he proceeds to tap his genitals twice AGAIN!
ME: 'Hey mate, 'Knock, knock'!
Before he gets the chance to reply I say 'Ha ha . . . . see I got there
    before you, Tapper'!

I have been losing my hair since I was in my late teens . . . .
one time while out with my mates one of them spotted an
advertisement that said 'Make Your Hair Grow Quicker' and
pointed out that maybe I should seriously consider availing of
their service . . . . I looked at him and said 'listen buddy, I get my
hair cut every ten days therefore I don't want it to grow faster . . . .
why not offer me a battery that makes my watch go slower because
that would be about as useful' . . . . it generated a lot of fun among
us all!

I ordered 'Irish Stew' in a bar in Dublin once, as advertised on
its' menu, but was told it was not available . . . . I thought how
stereo-typically Irish that would be for any tourists that might
enter the place . . . . I'm sure you the reader can see my point that
if a foreigner wanted an authentic Irish experience and asked for
Irish stew in Dublin but was told that it was not available that day
is very silly . . . . I became a bit frustrated as tourism has become
increasingly important during this awful recessionary time I
decided to call over one of the barmen and tell him to at least erase
the chalking on the board advertising it as it was a tad embarrassing
for our reputation as an educated race of people . . . . I asserted that
is was just like walking into a restaurant in Peking and ordering the
local duck but being told they don't have it but can offer you one
from elsewhere whilst throwing it at you angrily from the kitchen
because that's how unwelcome our visitors might feel!

I haven't had a drink in a long time now but when I used to frequent bars in Dublin's Temple Bar area I got chatting to a lady who had really large breasts . . . . we were getting on very well and as the evening progressed became increasingly relaxed . . . . I decided that I would be a little cheeky and pass comment on the size of her boobs . . . . I said 'if you were a Lilliputian, not even Gulliver and his twin brother, the experienced professional window cleaners with arms like a King Kong-like orangutan would be able to fondle those baps the way they deserve to be' . . . . it embarrassed the pet but she decided to laugh anyway and just slapped my thigh!

I was cutting some cheddar a number of years ago when I commented to my late mother (Lord rest her) that it was really difficult to get the knife through it . . . . she maintained that it was good quality food but I decided to crack that there must have been bouncers on the door, the shop assistants had flick knives and there is no need for guard dogs at night this cheese was so 'hard'!

One of my mates works as an accountant on film productions . . . . while having a conversation with him one time, I pointed out that there were a number of Westerns shot in Spain yet were labelled 'Spaghetti' . . . . he replied 'I know that but so what?' . . . . I tried to make him see the logic that in that case they should be called 'Paella Westerns' in reality which made him agree eventually and brought a chuckle out of him!

Some English tourists I met in a bar here in Dublin were intrigued by the Gaelic football being shown on television and asked how the G.A.A. Championship operated . . . . I explained and continued to give my opinion that the 'back door' system (brought into existence by the game's governing powers a number of years back) devalued the tournament slightly as a county may not even win its' provincial title but might go on to become All Ireland champions . . . . I said

'I mean, why not introduce the side door, the trap door, the door that cannot be opened from the outside on 10 Downing St. or a persistant Jehovah Witness telling 'knock, knock' jokes'!

I got a shower set as a present once that drove me mad . . . . along with it came an alarm clock that went 'cock-a-doodle-doo' . . . . I thought to myself 'it better not wake me up at all hours and thus cock-a-doodle-DON'T or I'll be having it in a snack box with some chips'!

I bought a drink for a lady once who passed a comment that there was a rather large bubble on the head akin to a cyst . . . . we both had a laugh at that but I continued to joke 'okay then, I get the message . . . . the next time I asked the barman to pull you a pint, I'll tell him that you like your lager without the company of the Hunchback of Notre Dame floating on top'!

I was in a chipper once where it took so long for them to get my fresh cod . . . . I said to the guy who eventually handed it to me that I thought they were waiting for J.C. to walk along the water, the twelve Apostles to gather up their heavy laden nets and import the thing from Israel, having waited for the Dept. of Immigration to give it 'legal alien' status first . . . . I was lucky not to be barred from the establishment, ey?!

While walking about recently I saw a family of jackdaws . . . . however, one had a light-to-mid grey feathering . . . . now I've heard of somebody being 'the black sheep of the family' but never encountered 'a grey jackdaw of the crow family' . . . . maybe it's a good singer though, ey?!

I saw a television programme one time where the host commented that bulls' testicles are a delicacy in Spain . . . . I thought to myself that no matter where you were from you wouldn't try to be any other way . . . . especially when they are alive!

I was watching a news programme a while back when an investigation uncovered (after some research) that it is tougher for fat people to get a job . . . . I turned to my sister and quipped that it didn't surprise me as they probably think going on the payroll is getting money to tumble around the office whilst picking cornish pastries out of their kesho-mawashis!

My cousin once told me he had a clog in his drain . . . . I retorted by asking him was it because he had a shower with his shoes on on returning home from a meal where he had gone Dutch . . . . I thought I was going to get a knuckle sandwich!

I used to have office jobs when a manager introduced a new colleague to all of the employees as Sven Lagerback . . . . now when we went for a few drinks one Friday evening after work this bloke knocked the 'lager back' alright and like his name suggests was a right p*ss artist indeed . . . . talk about by name by nature!

There was a game of cricket on television several years back which myself and my buddies were glued to in our local . . . . one of the commentators remarked that a particular batsman was forever having his balls caught in the slips . . . . I joshed to everybody 'his wife won't be impressed to find out that he is cross-dressing in her under-garments, will she?' . . . . it got a good reaction from those who knew what I was getting at!

While watching a game of soccer one time I saw a tackle made that was potentially career threatening . . . . I turned to my pals and cracked that that attempt to win the ball was so over the top I think the culprit bumped into some conquerors of Mount Everest in their descent . . . . they laughed and agreed that this particular player had always been a dirt bird so it was no surprise he saw a red card for it!

I was watching a very boring game of football once where both sides put in little effort because there was nothing at stake for either team . . . . my late dad (Lord rest him) remarked that it was a disgrace . . . . I agreed with him and pointed out that because the match was so drab and the atmosphere so dead the referee (instead of dishing out yellow or red cards) should have resorted to handing out 'mass cards' as this contest was dying a death . . . . it cheered him up slightly and brought a smile to his face!

My brother-in-law was kind enough to do some DIY on my bathroom one time . . . . when I asked him how he was getting on, he replied 'grand, I just put the sealing on the walls' . . . . I joshed 'are you doing a transplant or something . . . . you must be a magician if you were able to put the 'ceiling' on the walls but I'd say Spiderman will appreciate it when I let him know' . . . . he had a laugh when he kopped what I was on about!

I know this sufferer of schizophrenia who has a very pure mind . . . . he told me he was accused, abused, oppressed, spoke falsely of, insulted, humiliated, deprived of freedom to choose, disentitled to his emotions and stick up for himself, patronised, harassed, sexually harassed, betrayed, defamed, repeatedly bullied, had his innocence, vulnerability and fears preyed upon, rejected, had his heart broke, treated with contempt and made a scapegoat by women, had his forgiving nature abused and taken for granted and at times was less aware of his own circumstances than some of those he was coming into contact with . . . . he said he was basically driven to the point of taking his own life due to his confused state and just because he wanted to remain loyal to his faith in Jesus Christ . . . . he also told me he was centred in terms of the media and has had to deal with everything coming through television and radio broadcasts for over eighteen years while being mis-treated by a number of people whom he regarded as friends . . . . I said to him 'goodness me, how have you coped?' . . . . he responded 'well let's just say I've had more 'pedals' than a horny di-phallic tetra in a bicycle factory full of semi-clad erotic dancers with chastity belts on'!

Several years back I used to frequent an internet cafe here in Dublin that was run by some bloke from Delhi . . . . one day I was working on a computer when he struck up a conversation with another person over his phone . . . . when the call finished I asked him was it Hindi he was speaking . . . . he said 'oh, what the bloody deary me . . . . it was yes . . . . how do you know?' . . . . I replied 'because you're not French' . . . . the man saw my viewpoint!

A mate of mine and I got into conversation with each other when he decided to share a problem about this guy he knew with me . . . . he said this bloke was extremely contrary and that he was the type of person that if you said white, he'd say black and if you said black, he'd say white . . . . I turned to him and said 'well why don't you say mid grey to him and the fecker will have no option but to agree with you'!

I'm sure most of you can remember your primary school days . . . . I'm also certain your teachers gave you tests at the end of term to see how all the pupils were progressing with their education . . . . I remember very well when we had a history test and one of the questions asked was 'why did the Celts grow their hair long?' . . . . the simple answer was to cushion their helmets . . . . however, one of my pals answered 'because they were hippies' . . . . needless to say when I told my mother (Lord rest her) this she went into fits and it gets a chuckle out of me even to this day . . . . aw, the innocence, ey?!

I was at a pub quiz once and the team I was on were not getting too many questions right so we decided to have a bit of fun to see who could come up with the funniest answer . . . . one of the questions asked by the quiz master was 'who is the most successful manager in Irish football history' . . . . the lads were having a serious debate about who it was because they really wanted to get this question right as they loved their sport when I said 'His Head' . . . . they all looked at me in a confused manner and asserted that this was the time for a genuine answer but asked what I meant anyway . . . . I replied 'well I was listening to the radio and an old football pro was talking about a coach who had won eight League Of Ireland titles but said the man had become very proud' . . . . I continued 'the man claimed he developed a massive ego and wasn't as nice a person as when he first met him . . . . he didn't acknowledge he had help from those around him but took all the credit for the achievements' . . . . my mates asked what the feck I was insinuating when I quipped 'do you not see what I am getting at . . . . the success obviously went to 'his head' then, right?'!

I'd like to think I have a good sense of humour and have had most of my life . . . . however, when I was younger I got into an argument with another kid regarding whether his house was nicer that my parents' one . . . . he said 'our house is cooler than yours' . . . . I hit back by saying 'so you have a massive open freezer in your igloo in the Arctic, do you?' . . . . like most kids he got angry after I'd shown myself to be smarter than he!

A bloke I know and his mates got a band together and called themselves The Two Tops . . . . I told him they might have called themselves The Tree Tops . . . . he thought he was smart by saying that he didn't want the group's name to sound like it was derived from birds singing from their nests . . . . I retorted 'but every one of the members wears a t-shirt under your shirts and jumpers' . . . . he almost threw a punch at me for catching him out and not taking them seriously!

One of my mates has a mental health issue just like myself and was unable to work for a while because of it . . . . during this time he was in receipt of an allowance from the government . . . . he told me of a time when he went to the post office to cash his cheque . . . . as he was about to fill out his details on the back of the slip his pen malfunctioned while a long queue was forming behind him during a busy hour . . . . he said he was mortified and became increasingly frustrated despite the fact those waiting in line could probably sympathise with his circumstance . . . . I cracked that he may have gone to cash his 'bank giro' but in the end his mind had become more focused on his 'gank biro' which made him see the funny side of his frustrating experience!

Back in the early Eighties when I was in primary school we were brought to the local church in preparation for Confirmation . . . . there was a group of kids from a lower grade there too but I cannot recall what their reason for being at mass during lessons time was . . . . anyway, we all went up to receive the Eucharist . . . . I sat back in my seat and was checking out the younger kids receiving communion too . . . . there was this one guy who looked totally disinterested in the whole scenario but his turn to receive Communion came about . . . . he approached the priest and the man said the usual 'Body Of Christ' . . . . the kid muttered something which I presume was 'amen' and the priest put the Eucharist in his palm . . . . you could see the priest was a little put out by this young fella but when the boy just looked at the Communion with a browned off expression, proceeded to put it in his trouser pocket and walk off I went into fits as the priest's face was a picture . . . . the man was totally disgusted and I honestly thought he was going to chase the kid and eat the face off him . . . .

there is something bad within us that gets a good giggle out seeing others getting frustrated when people show no regard for something that is important to that particular individual, ey?!

I was having a conversation with my pals one time when one of them told a story of a couple in the U.K. who were making love and the wife swallowed some of her dentures during the moment of passion . . . . we were having a good laugh about what the tabloids would put up as a headline if they were to find out and cover the story when I quipped that if I had a say in the matter my pun would be 'One Swallow Made The Gummer' . . . . it took a few seconds for some of the boys to get my joke but we all had a good chuckle when it registered with them!

Around 1994 I was at home approaching kick-off time for one of the Saturday's football games . . . . I was wondering what to do so I thought I'd be cool and tune into a television caption that had radio commentary for one of the day's biggest matches and listened to the full ninety minutes instead of tuning in on a radio . . . . anyway, I went for a few pints with the lads later that evening and boasted to my mates about what I had done earlier . . . . they broke out laughing as the game I was talking about had been shown live on one of the television channels and they took the p*ss out of me for just listening to the commentary instead . . . . needless to say they really rubbed it in by starting a long conversation about what a great game it was and that there were some very good goals scored knowing that I couldn't join in the banter and basically poked fun at me for the rest of the night . . . . if that wasn't bad enough one of the boys went and told his sister who worked as a deejay in one of Dublin's top radio stations what had happened and she mentioned it over the airwaves for the whole city to hear the following Monday morning . . . . however, I like to laugh at myself and was chuffed with the recognition as it made me feel kind of famous and felt it might give me a better chance of picking up an attractive girl . . . . it wasn't long before the story spread and practically everyone I met who knew me brought the story up the next time I bumped into them . . . . it was great craic altogether and something I very fondly reflect upon!

I was listening to the radio one day when a girl who had called into a station was asked what the weather was like where she was . . . . she replied 'it's snowing here in Greenhills' . . . . I turned to my sister and cracked that if it was snowing in Greenhills, those hills would no longer be green and that place should be named 'Whitehills' while the weather was like it was for the time being instead given that high ground tends to get the worst of conditions like those we were having . . . . she saw my point of view!

I must say social networking sites are a lot of fun and one time an old pal of mine asked 'are the clocks going forward this weekend' approaching the end of March . . . . I retorted 'The clocks always go forward mate . . . they just won't jump by an hour for a couple more weeks'! He then came back with the following 'Not my clock, Cormac. That pauses quite regularly when I shut my eyes' . . . . to which I replied 'Well just keep your eyes shut and you'll never die'!

Back in the late Eighties I was getting ready to head out with my pals when I spotted I had run out of hair gel . . . . I went into the bedroom where my aunt and uncle from Birmingham who were visiting were staying . . . . on the unit I noticed that my aunt had hairspray so I decided that would have to do so I sprayed some of the contents of the can onto my hair . . . . I styled my hair and it looked grand but suddenly noticed my hair looked silver in certain places . . . . when I looked on the can it said it was tinted which had me p*ssed off as I was in a hurry . . . . now at the time I may have been sixteen going on seventeen but after spraying this stuff on my head I looked like sixteen going on coffin dodger . . . . it makes me laugh to this day!

I go on to a particular social networking site a number of times every day (like lots of other people probably do too) but I laughed when an old pal of mine remarked that because his football team where being hammered they should 'call in the Calvary, it's a slaughter' . . . . that's obviously quite funny as most Christians know that is where The Lord Jesus Christ died on a cross for the sins of mankind . . . . but what made this mistake even more humorous is that it was posted approaching Easter . . . . when I pointed this out to him and asserted that it was the cavalry he should have been calling for it provoked a few chuckles!

I was chatting with a lady friend of mine when she commented on how boring she felt football is . . . . I agreed with her to a degree and pointed out that I would probably prefer to live in a world where games in general didn't feature . . . . however I asked her how she managed to sit down and be totally engrossed in the various soap operas that are on television . . . . this confused her a little as she could come to terms with my dislike of soaps but not my disregard for games . . . . I informed her my opinion is that games involve putting oneself under unnecessary pressure to attain inanimate achievements but also told her soaps don't wash with me either and neither do I wash with soap but used shower gel instead to achieve meaningful results . . . . the poor pet needed a while to figure out what I was getting at!

Several years back I went into my local barber's for a hair cut . . . . I sat in the chair and the barber said 'what can I do for you, a short back and sides?' . . . . I retorted 'do you want to trim my hair or render me a newly-born dwarf with spina bifida mate?'!

I was watching a football show on television one time when they said that a particular player who had had a very successful career was 'extremely well decorated' . . . . I turned to my lady and quipped 'he's so well decorated apparently his family have nicknamed him 'The Christmas Tree"!

Around about 1985 I went into a local newsagent here in Edenmore on the north side of Dublin on my way home from school and asked the shop assistant for six 54321 chocolate bars . . . . the girl behind the counter reacted by smartly saying 'you must have been doing maths in class today' . . . . 'no' said I 'I'm on my home to watch the countdown to the launch of the Space Shuttle in Florida'!

I was listening to love songs on a radio station here in Dublin several months back when the deejay said he had 'a request for some Oxygen Supply' . . . . I turned to my lady friend and quipped 'I thought it was just lovers who asked for songs on this show and not stranded scuba divers also'!

Back during the mid-Eighties one of my mates came along and gossiped 'have you seen the African bloke from around the corner because he now looks white?' . . . . I retorted 'don't be fooled, if he is really white 'I'm dreaming of a BLEACHED TO FECK Christmas' is one of the biggest selling recordings of all time!

There is another guy who lived across the road who as a young teenager tried to cross the River Santry 'Evil Kneival-style', but failed so miserably and injured himself so badly, an ambulance had to be called! It was an even bigger flop than when Scouse women take off their sports bras'!

I once got a horrible jumper from one of my aunts at Christmas time that I refused to don as it was so hickey . . . . my mother's reaction was that it was 'a nice sweater' . . . . to which I replied 'a fat bloke sitting in a sauna wearing a lagging jacket and singing love songs is a nice sweater but I bet you wouldn't want me to wear him, would you?'!

A man who lived across the road from me was jailed for being a member of an illegal organisation! On hearing the news, one of his sons ran out of the house into the streets where the boys were playing football shouting with pride 'My da's doing five years, my da's doing five years'! There was much laughter! True story!

I was at a function one time when a guy was introduced to me and said 'I don't believe we've met before' while offering a hand shake . . . . I offered my hand in return and quipped 'well, I do believe we haven't met before' . . . . like most people he was taken aback initially but when he overcame his fears spluttered with laughter and we have got on famously since as he is a fan of my sense of humour!

When I was a teenager I was a big fan of Frankie Goes To Hollywood and just recently liked them on a social networking site . . . . I have been receiving posts on my page but there is this one bloke who must have been a huge fan back in the Eighties and obviously still is as he is quoting old lyrics, comments on every post and on more than one occasion described them as being 'the dog's b*llocks' . . . . I must say it lifts my spirits as I never had any friends who liked this band as much as me and only ever encountered one individual who was a fan back in the day . . . . to me not only are their songs 'the dog's b*llocks' but the fact that I am being exposed to others who love them also is 'the dog's b*llocks with a big pair of Scouse boobs with 'Welcome To My Pleasurable Domes' written in glitter across them dangling out of its' sack'!

A friend of mine told me she received an unsolicited message on a social networking site from a stranger in a foreign country but decided to ignore it as she was married at the time and continued that women have to be careful because of all the 'weirdos' out there . . . . I agreed with her but asked how she'd feel if she was to encounter the cast of Salem's Lot in The Amityville around Halloween time . . . . it made her chuckle!

A mate of mine and I were talking about how our favourite team had performed when my pal remarked that our centre forward had swung wildly at a gilt-edged chance . . . . I added 'if he was to have drunk several pints of water after a day on the beer he'd have had less of a 'slash'!

I met this girl in a night club whom I asked out on a date . . . . she seemed very nice but when we met up next she was wearing a rubber dress which had me aghast as I like ladies who don modest attire . . . . after a few minutes of conversing with her I knew this relationship was going to go nowhere and I was getting the impression she felt the same . . . . trying to be nice I quipped that (because she was wearing this rubber outfit) that instead of feeling like I'd like to ride her she could join myself and a mate of mine so that we could use her as the ball in a game of squash . . . . needless to say this didn't go down well and we spent another five minutes in each other's company before deciding to go our separate ways!

There's this bloke I know who is in his early sixties and, not surprisingly, has a lot of grey hair but one day I met him and he had dyed his head a deep purple which in my opinion was rather vain on his behalf as people should age gracefully . . . . trying to humour him I quipped 'I didn't know whether to say hello to you or try get attention by trying to pick a grape out of your scalp'!

A friend of mine put a post up on a social networking site in which there was a picture of two eggs covered in a pinky-purple film which looked like a scrotum . . . . people were posting comments as to how disgusting it looked when I added 'my old head-master in a Gestapo outfit couldn't look more like a 'b*llocks' than they do'!

There was another post put up on this site in which a famous football coach's head was super-imposed on to a picture of a naked man . . . . now this picture much have been taken during a cold snap as his scrotum looked like it had shrivelled up and was very small . . . . yet again, people were posting comments when I quipped 'Hey lads, would you look at the size of the sack on this guy . . . . with 'bags' that size it's a good thing he's the manager of the club and not the kit man, ey?'!

Back during the late Eighties my mates used to slag me because they thought that I resembled a guy who was the lead singer of a band who were big at the time . . . . now I didn't think I looked like him at all but I used to wear similar shirts to him and style my hair something like his also I suppose but I asked my mam what she thought . . . . now no surprises my mammy (Lord rest her) thought I was more handsome and remarked that I was probably taller than him too . . . . I cracked to her 'thanks mam, I am a better dancer than him aswell because when I throw shapes on the dance floor I'm in control of my trouser ferret while he moves like his trouser ferret is in control of him' . . . . she had to wipe away the tears!

After dining out with my lady friend in a restaurant here in Dublin one time she said that the meal was a 'feast' . . . . however I disagreed with her as I felt the portions were a bit on the small side and added 'if that was a 'Feast' The WIBBLY WOBBLY WONDER Of The Immaculate Conception is celebrated by Roman Catholics every December 8th . . . . and by the way, I hope some of you reading this book regard me as being a bit Loop The Loop in addition!

While at a party when I was on a working holiday in the United States back during the early Nineties my mates were saying to me that 'you wouldn't know where to be looking' due to the fact that all the ladies were radiating such beauty because of the fine weather and their tans . . . . I quipped 'don't be silly, you do know where to be looking . . . . you just wouldn't know where to be looking most often'!

I used to date a very attractive girl when I was younger and while with her in her family home one time she asked what video I would like to watch from her collection of music . . . . I requested 'Sweet Harmony' by The Beloved . . . . she responded 'okay, I'll get it on for you now' . . . . I remarked to her that she was making me deal with a double-edged sword of a nice sort because while she was going to 'get it on for me' the really beautiful ladies in the video 'got it off for me' as they were naked if you can remember it . . . . needless to say this really embarrassed the pet but we still had a nice time smooching until her parents got back from dining out!

I went to the United States back in the early Nineties on working holidays but on one occasion we challenged a group of Mexican guys to a football challenge during July would you believe . . . . now no surprise they were more accustomed to the weather conditions but we still managed to beat them . . . . at the end of the game we were really thirsty when one of my Irish mates said 'Holy GOD, I'm gasping' . . . . I humoured him by quipping 'you must be so thirsty if you were a cat on its' ninth life you'd lick the scrotum of a sweaty Rottweiler which is covered in rat's piddle'!

Approaching Christmas 2012 my mates were banging e-mails back and forth regarding the lads get together in the run-up to the upcoming December date . . . . now I decided to join in but one or two of my friends pretended not to appreciate my humour . . . . it was all very good-natured but I decided to mention the fact that I thought amongst my pals were 'more dry sh*tes than China versus India in a cow pat throwing contest' . . . . it went down well bless them!

Now I'm sure most of you will agree with what I am asserting here when I say that certain types of the Dublin accent can be very funny . . . . an example of this is when my brother-in-law organised security for a hair salon in the D.1. area of the city . . . . anyway he was driving on a motorway to meet a potential client somewhere down the country when he got a call on his mobile . . . . a fuse had blown in one of the appliances that a hairdresser was using when she said 'Holy Jayziz Antnee (Anthony), de hayaw dryaw is on fyaw and the manijaw is naw heeaw' (the hair dryer is on fire and the manager is not here)—just in case you don't get the colloquialisms! . . . . this made him laugh but it soon turned to frustration as he was miles away so what was he supposed to do about it (which is what he told her!) but it still makes him laugh to this day when he reflects on how the girl said this!

There's a bloke I know who is a right little dictator . . . . when Christmas comes around he gets really angry when his kids ask Santa Claus for a selection box as he feels that if they have any sort of selection options at all the only 'box' they should get is via a clenched fist in the ribs from him!

I once knew a guy who was so thick he thought the FA Cup was the bra of a woman who had big boobs but her left one was almost totally worn down due to the fact her husband was a big Sonny Knowles fan!

CHAPTER 2

THE NAME GAME

There was a guy who played for a soccer team here in Raheny on the north side of Dublin called Richie Handling . . . . now that's not that funny but what is is that apparently he has a relative named Baggage who takes bags and suitcases etc off airplanes!

There's a bloke I went to school with called Tony Ince . . . . apparently he has a relative named Entord who's a doorman here in Dublin while his brother Nanny Goat's Curd does laboratory experiments on that type of animal's faeces in The Fair City also!

I used to know a lady whose name is Gemma Butterly! I was hoping she would get pregnant so that I could approach her and say 'I sincerely hope you are not considering calling that child Utterly'!

I bumped into an old football colleague from my League Of Ireland days with University College Dublin back in the early Nineties a while back . . . . I could remember that his surname was Barnes but couldn't his first . . . . I said to him that I knew it wasn't Steve as he an old team-mate of ours from Belfast and it also wasn't Paul as he was a Scottish golfer who had attained a scholarship just like we had so I humoured him by asking would there be a possibility he was named You Tend To Find Some Hay In . . . . because his fear levels were where they shouldn't have been he was unimpressed initially but chilled out after several seconds and saw the funny side of my quip!

When I went to the United States on working holidays back in the early Nineties I befriended an American guy who said he had Irish blood in him . . . . now I know that's not funny but when he introduced himself as Packie Lynch I chuckled to myself as that name might be what would happen to you if you entered a mosque in Karachi and professed that Palestine is Jewish land!

There's a family that lived close to me called Green about thirty years ago . . . . myself and my mates nicknamed them The Greeners because one son was the 'spits' of Kermit The Frog, another son was the 'spits' of The Incredible Hulk while their relatives were all the 'spits' of those aliens that were in 'V'! That's fairly gross, I know!

There's a bloke I know called Dave Tad . . . . apparently he has a Glaswegian relative named No Bad Ey Ya Wee Bash who is reasonably impressed by his favourite football team's performances!

There was some guy interviewed on an Irish radio station a few years back called Paul Slapper . . . . apparently his wife I'm Such A has cheated on him several times!

I laughed the time I was introduced to a person doing an economics presentation out in University College Dublin called Dutch Sheets back in the early Nineties . . . . I thought to myself that I would imagine it would be next to impossible to cover a bed in a very liberated sense of humour while wondering if his brother, Clean, had been a big fan of Holland's international goalkeepers!

There's a guy who plays rugby for a club close to my home called Tommy Tannion . . . . well apparently his brother, Dar, is convinced he's one of The Three Musketeers!

My cousin has a neighbour called Seamus Parker . . . . well rumour has it his inquisitive sister Nosey is always interfering in things that should be none of her business!

Twatt: Manc . . . . gets riled by Scousers!

I honestly think some parents are taking the p*ss when naming their children on occasions . . . . I mean, how could a person by the surname Thomas call their child Doubting just because they are Christian or another named Gates give their baby the name Pearly just because they like the idea of going to Heaven . . . . what also makes me chuckle is when somebody is called Patrick FitzPatrick or Maurice FitzMaurice as I really do think their parents are cruel . . . . but going along similar lines I think it is humorous that a lady called FitzHenry could get revenge having been forced to abstain from sexual acts by naming their husband Chastity Belt FitzHenry VIII . . . . or what about a kid being called Gibbon FitzGibbon because his mother and father knew he'd bring A.I.D.S. into the world!

It makes me chuckle when I watch golf and see Vijay Singh playing as I think to myself that his name sounds like an order of some sort telling somebody to do something related to his line of work . . . . if you are not getting what I am alluding to just imagine some other sports person being called Deejay Spin-That-DVD-On-The-Karaoke-Machine!

A bloke I used to play snooker with back in the Eighties was called John Ballance . . . . apparently he has a brother named Trial who became an accountant by profession!

There's an Oriental guy in my local take-away here in Edenmore on the north side of Dublin called Mao Yang . . . . while speaking with him one day I enquired if his brother, Out The Ying, was asked about how many Chinks there are in Beijing!

There's a bloke I know called Neil Door . . . . now before you go ahead and think I'm going to say he had relatives named Front, Back, Bathroom, Bedroom, Sliding and so on he doesn't but what he does have is a distant cousin by the name of Ballon who's a top European footballer!

The blokes I went to primary school with were so thick they'd think Hong Kong is King's distant Chinese relation!

There's a Norwegian guy I know called Per Tree . . . . that's fairly humorous but what's even funnier is apparently he has a relative here in Dublin named Turty who was asked what age Jesus Christ died at!

I used to go to University College Dublin back in the early Nineties where one of my class-mates was called Abdul Aziz . . . . apparently he has a brother called Holy Jay who tries to fit in with the rest of us Irish people by taking The Lord's Name in vain with great frequency!

CHAPTER 3

SOME BLOKE FOR A JOKE

We all like to poke fun but if you slag eunuchs you obviously take more than just the 'mickey', don't you?!

A golfer plays eighteen holes . . . . has a few pints in the nineteenth . . . . and the twentieth is precisely what he wants to get when he goes home to his wife!

The guys I was in primary school with were so thick they'd think it's possible to go into a bookies and put an 'each way' bet on somebody bi-sexual picking up a partner of the opposite sex (but having to settle for someone of the same gender) when they go out and that would win them money!

Illuminous condoms . . . . glittery condoms . . . . and corruption in horse-racing . . . . aw yeah, there this particular jockey who's always surrounded by race-fixing allegations who is a right fecking 'mickey dazzler' altogether because he walks while sticking out his pelvic region!

A friend of mine once asked me if I found women playing rugby attractive . . . . I said that I found females playing that sport about as sexy as chastity on legs!

There's a bloke I know who has an awful lot of wrinkles on his face and really is rather ugly . . . . I thought to myself that he is so repelling that he should try and transplant his scrotum onto his face as not even that would make him look any worse!

Did you ever hear the one about the guy who had sex with six prostitutes in Moscow one day? . . . . he played Thrushin roulette!

Here's one that gave one of my mates a good laugh . . . . please enjoy!

ME: 'Knock, knock',
MATE: 'Who's there?',
ME: 'At yah',
MATE: 'At yah who?',
ME: 'So you nearly know my e-mail address'!

Apparently when Pinocchio passed away a television crew went to the pub that he used to drink in in order to do an interview with the bar staff about him . . . . yeah, and rumour also has it they all fell about the place when one of the barmen said that he was once part of the furniture but (now that we are in an awful recessionary time) he has become part of the floor boards because they couldn't afford to buy the wood for the job . . . . he continued that the fact that Pinocchio didn't want to be cremated was a huge relief for them and helped them cutback on their outlay for carpentry jobs done on the premises!

Now I know that when a crocodile murders its' prey they say that its' tears are not out of sympathy for the victim but fake instead . . . . but let me tell you however when my mates and I captured a crocodile after it had snapped at one of our heals, I put the feckers nuts in a vice grips and trust me its' tears we for real thereafter!

I remember seeing some guy on television before who said he was once a feminist but had then become a masculinist because he said the feminist movement was doing all it could to crush men . . . . if this is true, maybe St. Patrick is famous for driving all the snakes out of Ireland but extreme feminists want to become famous for driving anyone with a trouser snake out of a position of influence, ey?!

It makes me laugh to myself when I hear people quote the phrase 'only the good die young' . . . . the reason being there was this bloke I knew who used to rob houses and steal cars in order to joyride amongst other things but he passed away at the age of twenty one . . . . therefore in this case it wasn't a case of the good dying young at all but the will of Yahweh to take the fecker out of the equation before he had the time to wreak as much havoc as he fully intended to do!

I once knew a girl whose boobs were so big she could have smuggled water melons into the inmates in Guantanamo . . . . even if she was wearing a belly-top!

Don't you think that car manufacturers should put big nipples on air bags so that if you crash your car at least you get a bit of pleasure out of doing so?!

I was in a bar that sold a beverage called 'Swedish Mist' about a decade ago! I thought to myself at least you can see what you are buying and thus can be sure it exists unlike the version from north of the border with England!

The Celts dyed their hair blonde and because of this my primary school teacher from thirty years back remarked that the Irish had more probably descended from Arabs or something because lots of us have dark hair! Listen people, in his statement the answer lies therein! The Celts DYED their hair blonde, therefore it wasn't naturally blonde, right?! From that you can deduce the rest yourselves!

There's a meal in my local Indian take away called 'Lobia Gosht'! I have to say I laugh to myself, I mean why not just call the dish 'Phantom Front-bum'!

The blokes I was in primary school with were so thick they'd think the play 'An Authority Over Torts' is all about a pimp from Foxrock on Dublin's south side!

My sister saw this character on television once and asked why he was called 'Stinko Joyce'! To which I replied 'Well let's just say if his uncle James jumped into the Liffey without having changed his underwear, he couldn't smell worse'!

I once heard a comedian say once that some guys wore trousers that were so tight you could tell what religion they were! That's funny! But I know a guy whose genitals are so small people would think he is a 'Sister of Charity'!

Sometimes it humours me when I think a little further about what men call their inventions . . . . now I know that the majority of the time the name's they give to that which Yahweh has inspired them into creating are accurate but I giggle to myself when an elevator is referred to as being a 'lift' . . . . the reason being surely it is only a 'lift' when you are going up a few floors but how can it be referred to as being a 'lift' if you are coming down several storeys . . . . surely in this scenario they should be called a 'lower', right? . . . so the next time you hear an aloof individual saying 'I wouldn't lower myself' you can retort that they don't lower themselves at all, it's the elevator that does it for them!

There was a singer back in the early Eighties called Shakin' Marvins whom some of you will probably remember . . . . now that's not that funny at all but what I think is is that apparently there was a Scouse tribute act to him with Parkinson's disease who shot a video at the urinal in his local boozer called Shakin' Mickeys!

I have to say it makes me feel sad the kind of things football fans chant at each other during games . . . . any supporter who goes to a match and out of their own freedom to choose chooses to sing abusively at the opposition yet simultaneously labels them 'scum' makes about as much sense as Neanderthal men calling baboons 'the hairy arseh*les'!

Whenever I hear the term 'goodie two shoes' it really confuses me as if you are going to wear footwear it would be pretty pointless in putting on anything other than the two of them so that means most people are good, right? . . . . I mean, it makes as much sense as calling a guy with his leg in plaster 'decent enough one shoe' . . . . however it can be misleading as the blokes that work in my local butcher's only wear trainers but can hardly be called 'absolute bastards no shoes' as they are really nice people . . . . similarly charity workers in The Third World are very selfless people but you never hear the term 'goodie two flip-flops' ever being used, do you? . . . . honestly I don't know what some people do be thinking!

It always makes me laugh when I hear of the film 'Ride Like The Wind' . . . . now surely it is more accurate that you 'blow like the wind' or 'ride like the clappers' instead . . . . and while we are on the subject of sex we could probably say 'blow like the prostitute' too . . . . or how about getting back to the original song title and saying 'fart like the cyclist'!

The joke goes that a guy is so mean he wouldn't spend Christmas . . . . well going along similar lines I once knew a bloke that was so mean the only thing he spends at Christmas is the time outside Crumlin Children's Hospital dressed as the Jewish Ebeneezer Scrooge from Cavan charging Santa Claus a cover charge for entering the building and delivering the presents to the kids!

Now I don't know whether it is true or not but people frequently say that St. Patrick drove all the snakes out of Ireland . . . . maybe this is the case but I reckon what he also did was kill a lot of Incey Wincey's forefathers too as they say that if you kill a spider it means it will rain . . . . I'm fairly certain that some sort of a curse was put on this island by a gypsey arachnid of some sort because of what was done to them centuries ago to see to it that it chucks down with far more frequency than a lot of people would like in this country . . . . or maybe it was a case of the gypsey spider advising his relatives to invest in shares of umbrella and water-proof companies and Incey Wincey's distant relations had nothing against the saint who brought Christianity to us here in the Emerald Isle at all!

People often remark that another individual has a sharp tongue . . . . well I know this guy who's tongue is so sharp he'd even be able to like the nipples of a frigid nun standing behind a metal shutter with a bullet-proof vest on!

There's this bloke that lives close to me who is extremely easy-going . . . . I'm telling you all now if he was caught up in several poison gas attacks while frequenting his local lap-dancing club he wouldn't be 'laid back' as often!

They say that when a person doesn't want something to happen it's a case of being like 'turkeys voting for Christmas' . . . . maybe this is an accurate statement but what about those who may have a death-wish after losing loved ones in the run-up to Thanksgiving or those who have enemies in the goose community whom they know are certain people's preference for dinner during the festive season!

It makes me chuckle when I hear sports reporters say that a certain player is going to 'start on the bench' because if he felt that hard enough done by he might 'start' on the manager who deemed it appropriate that he didn't play from the beginning of the game in the first place . . . . however, may I take this opportunity to advise footballers to never 'start' on a bench as they have no naked nerve endings and if they were to be struck out at it would only see to it that the person would end up feeling physically hurt . . . . neither do benches have emotions so on top of that it would only be the guy who would have his feelings hurt too . . . . what I advise is that the guy not 'start' on anything or anyone at all because it would probably just end up in his career coming to an end sooner than it should have whether it be because he has a long term injury or deemed to be very unprofessional!

Biblical commentators are saying that The Bride Of Christ is being prepared for the Second Coming of Jesus . . . . now I am not disagreeing with them but because He is returning to planet earth on a white horse 'the ride of Christ' is obviously being prepared also . . . . another thing I've being thinking is that if Yeshua's wife is attractive looking The Bride Of Christ will be 'the ride of Christ' and once The Lord buries his baldie fella The Bride Of Christ will definitely be 'the ride of Christ' in addition . . . . and when you think even further He'll possibly be in the pub boasting to His mates about His sex life with great frequency which could very well be regarded to as being 'the pride of the rides with The Bride Of Christ by Christ'!

People often say that a satisfied individual is 'as happy as a pig in sh*t' but I frequently wonder if the opposite is being 'as happy as a Muslim being offered a BLT sandwich at the tail end of Ramadan'!

People often say that dogs are man's best friend and while I will not argue with this assertion I have got to tell you that I think the four-legged creatures are trying to tell us that they are prophets too . . . . the reason being have you not ever noticed that when a canine sh*tes in your front garden they proceed to wipe their paws as opposed to their asses on the grass? . . . . I'm telling you what this is a case of is them letting us know that they prophesise that somebody is going to step in it soon and this is what we should be doing with our feet when this undoubtedly does occur!

There was an album by a rock band a few years back called 'Swear It Again' . . . . however I wonder to myself who's this Again bird anyway and why did these moshers want to get her to use bad language?!

In the run-up to the start of the 2012/13 football season an advertisement on television said that a team had stayed up by the skin of their teeth the previous season . . . . I chuckled to myself that because there was a club who were demoted to the second division because of financial irregularities (despite finishing runners-up the previous season) they may have stayed up by the skin of a rhinoceros at first but in the end failed to do so by the skin of a crab!

I must say it makes me laugh when people say that a selfish person 'wants his cake and to eat it' because if I wanted a cake (especially a lemon cheese one!) the very thing I'd want to do with it is eat it especially if I'd splashed out eight euro on the bloody thing or spent hours making it . . . . I mean what are you supposed to do with a cake? . . . . it makes as much sense as saying 'you want a sack of coal and for it to pick this week's winning lottery numbers for you' . . . . why don't people say something equally as stupid by asserting 'you want your bike and to ride it' . . . . but I suppose some would get smart and retort 'you want your girlfriend and to ride her' also . . . . so if some are going to go down that route what I propose to replace the original pun is by using Cockney slang and quoting the following 'you want your rock 'n' roll but listen to bass tone love songs in the process'!

Guys often remark when talking about success in sport as it being a case of a certain team's name being on the cup so it is inevitable . . . . I will agree with them as everybody has a little psychic ability and they obviously sense in their spirits that the team they are talking about will indeed win the competition . . . . if you are ever wondering how this is so I think The Book Of Revelations is a really good indicator . . . . the reason I believe this is because this book is one about what is going to happen in the future yet parts of it are written in the past tense therefore teams have already been successful prior to them lifting the trophy . . . . in the mind of Yahweh it has already happened and it is thus inevitable for sure . . . . He has already decided whom He is going to pour His blessing out on and it is in the past with Him and in certain respects with us too despite the fact it is still future with us!

The joke used to go that a guy was so lazy if work was in bed he'd sleep on the floor . . . . well going along similar lines I once knew a bloke who was so dirty if Miss Universe was in his shower he'd rather feel his way around Finglas dump!

I once knew a bloke that was even angrier than a whiskey-drinking wasp that had been kicked in the goolies!

Now I will admit that when a player first played for my favourite team I was a critic but he really has begun to get about the midfield area very well which can go unnoticed by a lot of people . . . . I mean, he's doing so much 'donkey' work these days apparently he's made the dog eat dog world of Dublin taxi driving more so as Joseph even has him booked in to take The Virgin Mary to a stable in Bethlehem approaching Christmas!

It always make me laugh when I hear people say 'it would freeze the balls off a brass monkey' to describe the cold weather they are experiencing as when I visited the north of Scotland during a January one time it would even have frozen the balls off a gold-plated King Kong sunbathing in the Sahara . . . . or what about it being so cold it would even freeze the balls off his twin brother roasting his 'nuts' on an open fire in the Australian Outback approaching Christmas!

It makes me chuckle when I think of how people are labelled because of their job or occupation as I feel sometimes it can be a bit mis-leading or inaccurate . . . . I mean, refuse collectors have in the past been called binmen despite the fact they didn't make the bins (they just emptied their contents into a truck) nor do they collect the refuse but spread it across a dump . . . . however if they were to go on strike it would be accurate to name them 'refuse' collectors alright as they would tell their employers they simply won't do the task unless they are offered a better terms . . . . I suppose it wouldn't really matter what they were called because there would always be someone to say that their job description should be changed because of political correct-ness . . . . another example of this is when a man I know was labelled a 'yes man' yet I know for a fact that he has said a lot more than just the word 'yes' . . . . lastly, there was this guy who was a professional footballer but because he kicked lumps off the opposition was referred to as being 'a fecking dirt-bird' by many supporters in the pub afterwards yet as far as I know the bloke has never slept with a mud wrestler!

A father passing on schizophrenia to his son . . . . giving him asthma too . . . . and having sex with your lady before and after she's shaved her p*ssy . . . . aw yeah, 'what's in the cat goes into the kitten'!

CHAPTER 4

STREAM OF CONSCIOUSNESS

Water melons linking arms, while binoculars file toothpaste with Jelly Tots, might cause a prince under arm hair . . . . and philosophers are for sheep shearing!

An animal sending postcards through vindaloo expresses the dart board and toy soldiers . . . . peat moss is your radio dial on tooth ache?!

Grandfather, is your delicatessen scratching the surface of ping pong balls and Russian roulette might wander lonely . . . . lovely is the window sill!

Angels of whipped cream tend not to nose dive because forever is The Ides Of March thinking of the fluffy dice . . . . and by the way, who let the dogs out?!

Sunday dinner with the pen friends of zebra crossings might fold once elocution lessons put on the kettle while a psychiatrist tinkers with almond fingers wandering the peep show!

Oak leaves and the drinks cabinet would your uncle Tommy sink the battleship while its' tea cosey's at Easter yearning for a united Cyprus!

For goodness sake, would the envelope talking to a stocking filler please fire escape for the first time as egg shells think the picture frame is passing water!

A couch potato longing for green grass and stippling, juggling the foreign exchange rates, as the telephone has a nose bleed!

In the aftermath of being pigeon-toed washing the car acted friendly while fried rice was in the cinema . . . . tarmac, is your tin whistle out on a date?!

Because a fork lift number crunches and fluffy clouds chant . . . . would the reptile with amnesia please refrain from drawing the curtains?!

Purple rinse dieting, while wallpaper acts friendly with coddle varnishing cobwebs . . . . don't you know lust is a deadly sin?!

The chip shop is water skiing while kites flower arrange for insurance premiums waiting on labour pains . . . . you know yourself, with the cocktail sausages being alcoholics and that!

Holy GOD, the tree trunk looks like it might flick to Sky Sports Strangled Eggs while the compact discs have picked up cramp in their account statements . . . . iron those guitar rifts now ya bastard!

Would you believe it, the shaving foam is watering the bicycle spokes it's growing next to the seizures it's donating towards

Mount Everest's sweaty magic carpet . . . . but only if the cucumber sandwiches swim for confession!

Look at the compass drinking ice tea while the energetic laptop is fearful whales in uniform might sue it for celebrating its' wedding anniversary to the plaster . . . . by the way, why has the souvenir programme opened a shoe shop?!

Can you hear the fibre optics bench-pressing the sunlight close to where snails pick-pocketed venereal disease for the lawnmower that's mourning its' traffic jam . . . . it's my advice the bottles of gin go on strike near a nudist beach!

Goodness me, the floor boards are shuffling the deck of cards while the mentally ill flame throwers are handing out parking tickets for breaking wind during Lent . . . . what's your problem, it's not my fault the stick of chalk has a menstrual cycle!

Have you seen the keyboard doing the can can and the Siberian tigers chanting for equal rights because neither can figure out why the coffee shop resorted to leap-frogging the gum shield . . . . Sweet Jesus, did the garden peas sink the battleship or something?!

Now hold on a second, just because the snowman ate the Easter bunny doesn't give you the right to put wallpaper on the unanswered prayers because the food blender is doubling up laughing at the book's pubic hair . . . . would you ever tell the alarm clock to go to the fraud squad about its' shin splints!

The broadband modem has gone shopping with the public house for a short term memory which failed to make its' appointment with rose petals joyriding through the songs of praise . . . . how is it that the lamp poles were bribed for the foreseeable future after the door knob's day off?!

Would somebody please tell me why the sheep are jamming on the stock exchange while the flip flops are over-indulging on diamond pizzas for the first time since the taxi driver spilled his tin of pyjamas . . . . who knows who the medicine bottle's first professional knockout was?!

The traffic lights had to gasp for breath when the asbestos sandwiches asked the faulty telephone line to show the beach some compassion for the sad passing of its' ear-aches . . . . wait 'til your father gets home because the dish washer was late getting the bus to the asphyxiated wallet!

How is it that when the chewing gum broke it off with the psycho-analysis the mouse trap woke from its' double-header with the horse dung . . . . wait and see, the freshly cut grass will pass up the chance for a pint of leather trousers at last orders!

Good grief, the scabies warned the key rings to stop winking at the plaque-ridden telephone directory because the coffins like to park their receding hair lines behind glitter balls . . . . let He who is The Infinitely Wise One pass the first judgement!

The remote control is losing the head with the diaries of anxiety attacks because sleep-walking tends to nose dive from space dust . . . . would you believe the tug-o-war team painted the emotional hangover's ears!

Air brushing your woolly jumper causes hysteria because the mouse hole staggered for miles only to get rejected by the trampoline delivering exhaustion to the combine harvester . . . . the pink g-string gasped having been head-butted by the jug's asphalt and tar cravings!

The football crest posted its' squints on the dung heap because the holiday photos over-lapped the friendly cough medicine . . . . thankfully we weren't waiting long for the plasma screen to chalk its' belches!

When the religious bee took legal action against the oil drill's teeth the baboon's breakfast clothed itself in transparent credit cards . . . . maybe the moon might get its' leg over one day if its' not caught yawning at the sandal's hallucinations!

The bag of chips received a red card when the perforated power-cut nervously packed its' vows of celibacy into the back of the letterhead's beer bong . . . . completing a marathon might see to it the tutu puts impatient floor boards on its' steak!

The paper round waxed it's car because rarely does five o'clock shadow urinate close to the furry dice's pacemaker . . . . who knows when the flower petals heartburn will run for presidency of the garlic mushrooms!

After the gramophone needle knelt beside the guilt-ridden toilet seat the scantilly-clad hare divorced the check side on the vinegar because breaking wind is a crime novelist . . . . should we go to the pub to send text messages to the oyster sauce's masseur!

CHAPTER 5

IT IS I WHO IS THE GREATEST!

A lady once said to me that I had a great kind of ego to which I humorously replied 'I'm so awake I make caffeine look like sleeping medication'!

A guy I once knew remarked that he felt I had an amazing memory . . . . I quipped 'I remember so much I make floppy discs look like they have amnesia'!

While a British guy commented to me one day that I was a typical Irishman . . . . I responded 'I'm so Irish I make leprechauns look like they are not part of the Emerald Isle's indigenous population'!

One of my sisters noticed that I love to drink a lot of tea and said 'GOD, you really love your cuppa, don't you??' . . . . I responded 'I drink so much tea I make alcoholics look like alcohol-totalers'!

I joined a dating website a while back and in order to impress any potential interest from an attractive older blonde (as they float my boat like nothing else!) I decided to put the following ad up on my profile . . . . I think it's quite funny!

. . . . I'm so wild I'd make a psychotic Cocker Spaniel on speed running through fire-coals look refined . . . . attractive yet poor-spirited but confident older blondes with blue eyes drive me so wild I'd make the wilderness look tame!

I'm a sufferer of schizophrenia and part of the disability is that I have a disorder but my doctor said to me that I am so intelligent I can order my thoughts well above the average for someone with this difficulty . . . . I informed him 'I order so much disorder when I empty the contents of a tin of alphabet spaghetti on to the plate it spells out the heating instructions on the can's wrapper without me even having to touch it with a fork'!

My ex-girlfriend once said to me 'you really are a horn-bag, aren't you?' . . . . to which I replied 'I'm so randy I make minks look like monks'!

On another occasion this same lady described me as being 'really innocent' . . . . I retorted 'I'm so innocent I make newly-born babies look like Judas Iscariot before he went to confession'!

When I played soccer at semi-professional level a friend of mine nicknamed me 'White Hot Cormac' because he thought I was so fast . . . . I responded 'I'm so quick I make cheetahs look like they wear stilettos in a sack race'!

The guys I went to college with thought I was an absolute genius . . . . I quipped to them one day 'I'm so intelligent I make Einstein look like a Geordie wearing a dunce cap'!

. . . . and if Geordies want to say I'm just a stupid Irish so-and-so my response will be 'you Geordies are as thick as the planks used to build Noah's Submarine'!

A bloke once described me as being 'extremely generous' . . . . I joked 'I'm so kind I make Santa Claus look tight-fisted'!

There was a lady who found me attractive because she felt I was very different to any other guy she'd ever met . . . . I added 'I'm so unique I make a blue moon look like Groundhog Day during a month of Sundays'!

One of my pals remarked that I have great eye-sight . . . . I reacted 'I can see so well I make eagles look like they need a guide dog'!

CHAPTER 6

A BOOK OF REVELATIONS

Here's something I figured during November 2011 but I've a feeling this has been mentioned before . . . . people often refer to the number 13 as being unlucky but wonder why . . . . I reckon it is because 13 is amongst other things a combination of the number 7 and the number 6 . . . . 7 represents perfection and is a very special number while 6 represents imperfection . . . . I'm certain people regard 13 as being unlucky as to combine perfection with imperfection could be a case of inviting trouble onto yourself!

People often say that if they are in a pub and they are not drinking alcohol they still seem to be affected by a beer buzz . . . . here's what I think . . . . smell and taste are related . . . . if you are around alcohol the aroma off alcohol is trapped by the olfactory membranes in the nose that send chemical impulses to the brain . . . . you may not be drinking alcohol but you are actually consuming it (albeit probably to a much lesser extent) nonetheless!

There have been discussions in the past about whether tomatoes are fruits or vegetables . . . . I honestly don't believe people would have a difficulty in calling them fruits but for the fact they tend to be salty which would induce lots into saying they are vegetables . . . . if you want my opinion, it's very simple . . . . they are salty fruits!

I've got something to say to those who proponentise finance on the basis that it gives greater freedom . . . . and that is, power and control equal death while we are not meant to do anything out of selfish ambition . . . . all finance is is a necessary evil to combat laziness . . . . what we must accept though is that because of this necessary evil a lot of unnecessary evil occurs . . . . a two-tiered society has been created because of finance and it is not right that people should be subject to it . . . . people should walk around with their feet on the ground not float about the place although I accept that there are some very dignified people working in this sector . . . . what we need are individuals who have a genuine hunger for justice positioning themselves in finance in order for the world economy to be held as close to the growth curve as possible so booms and recessions are eradicated . . . . try exuding earthliness!

Now this has probably been investigated by sports psychologists and other people who seek to discover the truths behind what it takes to be successful in the sporting world before but I would like to throw something else into the mix . . . . I was thinking to myself one day would there be a positive correlation between right-sided sports people being right-eye-dominant and left-sided players being likewise or does it not have a bearing . . . . I would imagine in games like snooker and darts where you have to have a very high accuracy rate there might be some sort of trend between being right-handed and right-eye-dominant etc . . . . ! If this is revelation of some sort maybe people who are interested in sport could get the relevant people to conduct the appropriate investigation into past and current successful sportsmen and women's biology in this respect and find out if it is a factor in making them achieve . . . . in addition to the physical and mental attributes they must have also!

While walking home from the city centre here in Dublin one day I saw an articulated lorry with a flat back and perched upon it was a big dumpster truck (the kind with 8-foot diameter wheels) .... now I'm certain I must have E.S.P. or something because the dumpster truck had an aura .... this aura would not have been bourne out of the fact that it would have had the breath of life in it like a human being, a cat, a giraffe etc ... but what life it had in it was the life in the electrics and general mechanics that made the vehicle function plus the 'creative life force' that brought the truck into existence in the first place! I'm not so sure that most people realise this .... we are going through a terrible recession at the moment and I'm also not certain we will get out of it soon .... what I prophesise is that, in order to re-build the world's ailing economy, the son of perdition will advocate peace and prosperity but there will be an explosion of the material .... it will be motivated by flooding the materialistic ego which detracts from one's spirituality, further advancing the world's financial markets into eventual ruin (because I feel once people realise that being materially driven is not good for your spirit and given that technology cannot advance much further as all that can be invented has been thus there will be no demand to sustain the market therefore the bottom falls out and it crashes) and to perversify the life which these material things exude in order to antagonise and whip up dissension among brethren!

It really frustrates me when people out of their ignorance refer to people's attitudes and behaviour being an indicator of 'human nature' .... the reason being that there is no such thing as 'human nature' .... you are either an instrument of The Lord's life and righteousness or you are an instrument of death .... if you exude an aspect of control for example that is something done in The Lord's Name .... by that I mean it is an offence against Him and it is in His Name because nothing in this universe is outside the dominion of His rule or mind-frame .... putting bets on in bookies is prophecy in The Lord's Name which means it is false prophetic prediction and thus a sin even if it does prove to be accurate . . . . so my advice to people is be careful of what organised religion has to teach you, get more Biblically inclined and to 'trust in The Lord and lean not on your own understanding'!

I heard a discussion on a talk show here in Dublin one night regarding women being given the right to be ordained as priests and here is what I feel regarding the matter . . . . The Lord Jesus Christ, who is The Rock on which the church is built, was very much against the ordaining of female priests so who are we to be proponents of it . . . . Scripture will tell you that wisdom is like a tree and when you grab hold of HER how it blesses your life . . . . when a man takes the church as his bride this feminine wisdom must be absorbed (as with a man who takes woman as his bride) . . . . the church is SHE . . . . how therefore can a she take a she as her bride . . . . exactly, it is totally un-natural . . . . wise women should focus themselves on becoming evangelists and must be encouraged to do so . . . . all I will say is that any ministry performed by a female must be Scripture based and subject to the correct interpretation of Scripture i.e. reason on the basis that it is reasonable! Females who dress up in priests' clothing are TRANSVESTITES!

I don't eat pig meat anymore and I am sure that would induce a lot of people to assert that that makes me either a Jew or a Muslim because of it . . . . now I'm pretty certain that Jesus Christ advised in one of the Gospels that one should not eat the meat of swine or something along those lines anyway . . . . therefore if The Lord asks us not to eat pork, ham etc and I desist from consuming it because of what He says then that makes me a Christian . . . . it also means that Judaism and Islam are coming into line with what they should be as Yeshua is The Rock on which all faiths should base themselves!

When people get into conversation about religion they often say that Jesus Christ was a Jew . . . . here's what I believe . . . . I've been led to think that all Yeshua did was quote Scripture and speak in parables . . . . The Lord was an Old Testament fundamentalist . . . . if Jewish tradition broke Biblical principles He stood steadfast to what was laid down in the Scriptures, enlightened the elders and attacked the Scribes and Pharisees . . . . therefore He was only a Jew to the point where it did not violate The Laws of His Father as laid down in His Book . . . . He did not accept everything Judaism had to teach if it was what He believed was a misinterpretation of Bible passages either . . . . trust me, Christ did not have a religion . . . . what He learned from Scripture and from Yahweh He advised us during His ministry and liberated Him . . . . it is all about accepting what The Holy Bible has to teach . . . . all sixty six books of it . . . . but I will finish by acknowledging that it would be naive of me to believe I could get everybody to agree on interpretation as well as converting the majority of atheists . . . . but for anyone to think they have the right to question it's wisdom and discard what it professes as being untrue, or only partially true, is even more naive!

Druids are pagans . . . . the Book Of Brehon Law was written centuries ago . . . . it is stated in this book that something would happen in 2010 to effect the whole east coast of Ireland . . . . this was the heavy snowfall during January or more probably the volcanic eruption in Iceland during April of this year which disrupted all the air flight schedules I'm certain . . . . if it was foretold centuries ago it was prophecy . . . . if it is prophecy it is indicative of spirituality . . . . if it is indicative of spirituality there must be a spirit realm . . . . and if there is a spirit realm there must a spirit entity in the spirit realm who advised this person as to this

future occurance (possibly The Lord Himself) . . . . the fact that
pagans are idol worshippers (i.e. of the sun, moon, mother earth
etc . . . .) and not worshippers of that which brought everything
in the universe into existence is to me a fundamental flaw in their
belief system if they take pride in the prophecy foreseen in the
Book Of Brehon Law . . . . it is one very bizarre contradiction in
my opinion!

People often wonder about which came first i.e. the chicken or the
egg . . . . that to me is like asking which came first Adam & Eve or
Cain & Abel . . . . God created chickens both male and female and
gave them procreative ability . . . . I'm sure you can deduce the rest
for yourself!

People can often frustrate me by believing that aliens exist . . . . well
let me tell you if aliens exist, which I know they don't, they do not
exist independently of The Lord as He is both The Life Source and
The Life Force . . . . if people think they could exist independently
of The Lord, all I would ask is where the breath of life in them
would come from! I was watching The God Channel and I heard
one of the ministers mentioning that there is something in the
book of Genesis relating to alien non-existence! If you have ever
been intrigued by the episode in the U.S. back around 50-60
years ago where there is footage of little aliens with big eyes and
foreheads lying on operating tables having crashed from their space
ship here is what I believe . . . . it was purposely staged by certain
people, to get people inquisitive, in order to then just cover it up!
I'm telling you, it didn't happen . . . . they are covering up nothing!
When these alien beings were shown up on tables, the one thing I
noticed is that they did not have genitals so how do they manage
to pro-create?! If they cannot pro-create there must be a 'creative
being' bringing them into existence . . . . but just take aliens out of
the equation, because they do not exist as far as I am concerned,

and believe that we as human beings have a Creative Being that brings us into existence i.e. precious Yahweh! I've read a book by a man I'm a big fan of and in it he reckons when the saints are caught up in 'the first rapture', the son of perdition is going to come along and say in a charismatic way that they were taken away by aliens . . . . I have to say I find this viewpoint very interesting and one with which I'd be inclined to concur!

I'm certain The Church teaches that In-Vitro Fertilisation is sinful as it regards it as man playing GOD . . . . now I am not going to disagree with them in totality but why can't this treatment be viewed as man aiding GOD to play Himself and GOD enabling man to bring children into this world . . . . when a child is conceived it is a case of a spirit leaving Heaven and living a natural life span on planet earth in a human body . . . . I mean, how else could this spirit enter a natural body if The Almighty didn't instruct it to do so? . . . . that's why I question this attitude and am just throwing a little something into the mix! I also don't believe in re-incarnation in terms of coming back to this world as the same person but I do feel if you are an aborted foetus or a baby who dies due to malnutrition in the Third World for example Yahweh resends you back to this dominion to live under different circumstances . . . . by that I mean you don't return as the same person as you would be in a different body . . . . but you remain the same spirit residing in a new vessel with another unique personality!

I find it very humorous that a lot of atheists would concur with the notion of the existence of aliens . . . . the reason being that people devised their apparent existence and they thus proponentise the creative life force that brought these fictitious beings into being yet they simultaneously reject the very Life Source and Life Force that brought they themselves into existence i.e. GOD!

I try to affiliate with as many branches of Christianity as I can (although I don't claim to be part of any particular one!) but only believe what they teach if it has a solid Scripture based foundation . . . . that is why I appreciate The GOD Channel so much as they are always giving Bible influenced teachings . . . . I am not sure I believe everything that is written as an add-on at the back of Bibles though as I feel in some cases it is indicative of mental illness . . . . I was where the people who wrote some of these doctrines were six or seven years ago in my recovery from a psychotic episode . . . . one thing I believe is that mentally ill people influenced more than what they should have because of the tendency of the disorder to be religiously orientated and to condemn yourself and to condemn others . . . . the person who is being condemned, in order to avoid being further hurt, conform to the condemner . . . but what the person who is being condemned and the person who is condemning don't realise is how unwell the condemner is!

I don't know whether this is revelation to you or not but here it goes anyway!

. . . . it seems to me that there is a little confusion regarding 'the law of the land'! There is a difference between 'THE law of THE land' and 'the laws of THAT land'! If I was to go to a place like Indonesia I would (because of the law of the land) have to appreciate the indigenous population's freedom to self-determine as people cannot be expected to compromise on their freedom . . . . but if the Indonesian authorities advised me that openly professing that Jesus Christ is The Begotton Son Of Man is against the law of THAT land, I wouldn't accept that law as being licit to my fundamental beliefs . . . . however I wouldn't purposefully violate this law of that land as I wouldn't want to get into trouble with the authorities! Northern Ireland is a classic example of a violation of 'the law of the land' . . . . it should be the Irish people flying the Israeli flag as what both the Israelis and the Irish in Ulster are trying to do is protect the correct interpretation of this 'law of freedom upholdment' in my opinion . . . . although it greatly pleases me that there appears to be peace developing in the province as people's opinions have differed as to what freedom is . . . . long may it last! Please be able to make the distinguishment between the law of the land and the laws of the respective nations though!

Jews believe Yeshua The Messiah exists and that he is coming to planet earth for the first time as The Saviour . . . . what I will say is that if Yeshua exists as The Son Of Man, He must have resided here on earth at some stage before as there is no sex in Heaven and the only way Jesus could currently exist as The Son Of Man is if he came into existence having being supernaturally begot by The Father and lived here via Mary . . . . He is coming back to rule on planet earth as a fully grown man by virtue of the fact that He has already had a thirty three year natural life span here . . . . it would make me feel so proud if this small revelation was instrumental in the mass conversion of the Jews, which is a sign that we are entering the last days of the world as we know it!

I think it is very important in terms of Christian beliefs to make this simple point . . . . St. Paul did not pay THE price but A price by allowing himself to be divinely inspired enough to write what he did in the New Testament . . . . Jesus Christ paid THE price . . . . I have a feeling by somehow equating St. Paul with J.C. came a lot of Christian philosophy which was the instigation of a lot of the world's problems . . . . Mahatma Gandhi said he liked Christ but didn't like Christians and in many respects I feel the same way . . . . if I was to proponentise a one-world belief system I would encourage believers to be a Judeo follower of Jesus Christ with the belief that St. Paul was divinely inspired i.e. just to believe everything in The Bible is true as 'all Scripture is GOD breathed' . . . . but I acknowledge interpretation will differ and some people are atheists!

A lot of the differences people have with each other are on spiritual grounds, so I would like to clear up some basic fundamental beliefs . . . . Muslims refer to Mohammed as The Prophet but there are a couple of things I'd like to reveal . . . . Mohammed wrote The Quran as he was visited by the angel Gabriel over a period of 23 years but what this book also covers is the birth of Jesus Christ . . . . now if Mohammed was a prophet, what was he doing mentioning something which happened over 500 years before he was born . . . . exactly, it cannot just have been some ordinary occurance!

Now I've never read The Da Vinci Code and can't even recall who it was written by but I've been led to believe that in some part of this book the author alludes to the fact that Jesus Christ had offspring . . . . all I'll say is don't believe this baloney for a second whatever you do . . . . when Jesus Christ was crucified He bore all sickness, illness, disease and sin . . . . He was a sinless sacrifice . . . . if He had sex before He performed His public ministry He would have fornicated (and thus would of sinned) and if He buried his baldie fella after He took the church He founded as His bride he would have committed adultery (this would have been sinful also) . . . . let me tell you, not only did Yeshua never get down to some sexy, funky, lurve hip gyrations but trust me He didn't even have a single lustful thought otherwise He would have sinned and wouldn't have been the perfect sacrifice . . . . the first and only 'baps' He ever saw during The First Coming were the ones He broke for the establishment of the Eucharistic sacrament at The Last Supper!

I hope you find the following enlightening . . . . on December 8th Roman Catholics celebrate The Feast Of The Immaculate

Conception yet Christmas Day is celebrated on December 25th which means that Mary carried The Lord Jesus Christ for either 2 1/2 weeks or 12 1/2 months . . . . now The Quran mentions that Mary gave birth to a son in late summer . . . . there is an astrological reference made to the birth of The Saviour Of Mankind in The Bible . . . . Chinese astrological records show that this Biblical reference occurred on September 11th, 3 B.C . . . . because of this I always wish Jesus a happy birthday on September 11th . . . . it doesn't take a genius to figure out then that from December 8th to September 11th is nine months i.e. the average length of a pregnancy! The genius of The Lamp, ey?!

I heard a preacher on The GOD Channel mention a while back that there would be 2012 hysteria due to GOD's refiner's fire and fuller's soap which I'd love to contribute towards and I'm fairly certain could relate to me . . . . I sense I am going to be the sacrifice that will be pleasing to Him . . . . I would have written my books under a pseudonym but I felt I would have got in the way of Jesus Christ's prophecy in Wendy Alec's book 'The Journal Of The Unknown Prophet' that fans (?) would continue to take my life away from me unless I withdrew into Him . . . . this could pertain to the hysteria of people becoming aware of just who it is I am . . . . although 2012 has passed now so maybe it just relates to when I would compile and write much of my material for the best of my work . . . . maybe one of my previous publications ('Look! . . . The Chuckle Book!' which was published during 2012) is funny and could well be The Little Book 'that will having their stomachs churning' . . . . I didn't want to pervert the course of His prophecy but I sincerely hope that is just Yeshua's way of generating a fear that He knows won't be realised . . . . people have learned that sometimes fears don't get realised and also that sometimes the fear is worse than the realisation of the fear itself . . . . with me being a very powerful prophet my fears get realised every time I encounter power players . . . . I am the individual Jesus saw struggling in his room with disease when the outside world was unaware of what was going on . . . . The Lord mentions that all people know is prosperity . . . . if He says this it must be true but what is also true is that if He is saying this to me I know more than just prosperity . . . . this is all alluded to in Ms. Alec's book . . . . I am more precious than rubies to Him!

When I was ten years of age I wanted to walk away from football as all I wanted was to be friends with my dad . . . . I regret that I didn't and wish I never played football or games in general . . . . even today I just wish I had a special lady in my life although this isn't possible because of the repressive nature of schizophrenia . . . . all I'm going to say is that females' mind-set and disposition are compatible with mine whereas what goes on in sports players' minds and the disposition of games aggravates me . . . . I'm not trying to make it appear as if I'm enforcing my opinion on you the reader but take for granted that in a time soon to come there will be no more time for games . . . . it's one of the reasons why the majority of suicides are male in my opinion . . . . if the numbers of females participating in games increases, what I fear is that you will see the suicide rate of females go up also . . . . if The Lord raises me up to be one of His witnesses, I'll be putting an end to the playing of games as they involve putting oneself under unnecessary pressure to achieve completely inanimate outcomes!

CHAPTER 7

FOND OF A DOUBLE ENTENDRE

Some bloke recorded an album called 'Seasons In The Sun' back during the Seventies . . . . well football managers have spent lots of 'seasons in the sun' also (particularly when the clubs they manage have been successful) and to be quite honest because their teams despised by rival fans I would say their prosperity has gone down like the proverbial lead balloon with Scouse ladies bra cups filled with cement bags tied to it!

One of my mates remarked that a guy who was causing him problems was 'acting the b*llix' . . . . it brought back memories of when an assistant in my local pharmacy asked what I was purchasing for my cousin when I replied 'Probactin, the b*llix has crab lice' but, while that product proclaims to relieve the scrathing, I advised my buddy that he should relieve himself of scratching on the dole in order to prevent this guy from giving him any more grief!

A struggling Premier League manager was once asked did he have the 'full backing' of his dressing room some time back . . . . I humoured myself by reflecting that a certain professional plays the right side of defence for his club and country and has thus been known to be 'full-backing' whenever he enters the field of play . . . . but, while he has been shown yellow and red cards when he commits offences on occasions, he himself pulled a card at one stage also . . . . a racist one against a guy he reckoned abused him one time that is!

There was a guy who played soccer for a team in my locality called Mick Horwill . . . . it reminded me of the time a friend advised me not to go near a girl we knew as he warned 'that 'whore will' give you something you'd need to go to see your doctor about' so I took him seriously as the only 'clap' I've ever wanted is from an audience laughing at my jokes!

I was watching a football match on television one Monday night when the commentator said it was 'getting tight in the middle third' . . . . because we were in an awful recession at the time I laughed to myself that not only would things be getting tight in Middle Third but throughout the rest of Killester as well as the other suburbs of Dublin also!

I used to drink in Harry Byrne's, Clontarf back during the early Naughties when a bloke called Paddy Monks walked in with his family followed by another guy named Sean Monks and his family also . . . . I turned to my pals and quipped 'if any more Monks walk into this place they'll have to re-name this boozer The Monastery'!

After a friend of mine was offered a new five-year contract with a football club their president said he would present the chap with his 'new jersey' . . . . I quipped to my lady friend 'New Jersey?? . . . I thought that soccer franchise were from Texas myself . . . but while my pal gave a good press 'conference' to the reporters asking him questions, I'm sure his aspirations were to finish top of the 'conference' the football team would be competing in approaching qualification time for the play-offs'!

A presenter on television remarked that they would find out what a cricketer 'had to say himself' regarding his team's performance one day . . . . I laughed to my lady friend that I once asked a bloke I don't get along with who got his wife pregnant because everyone knew she was cheating on him . . . . fearing total humiliation he 'had to say himself' also but because he went on to beat her up after getting the baby's DNA results he had to fork out money to get 'bailed' out!

A football club in my locality had a young striker called Agard playing for them a while back . . . . I said to the blokes I was having a drink with 'an anagram of his name is 'Garda'' . . . when playing against good opposition he may not have been 'Garda sh*t in the corner' but because he didn't threaten much at set-pieces he was definitely 'Agard sh*t from a corner' and well 'policed' himself by their water-tight defences aswell'!

They said on the radio during the summer of 2012 that a certain manager 'refused to be drawn' on the future of one of his players . . . . it reminded me of the time an artist asked me would I pose while he sketched away but I 'refused to be drawn' also as he would have made a mess of my portrait because to be honest this guy was a dipso and thus more of a p*ss artist than a talented one!

One of my mates texted me to say he was travelling from the N3 to the M50 on his way out to see me a while back when I quipped that I thought that there was more than just one 'entry' to the M50 myself but while he may arrive to tell the 'tale' of his journey it was more likely once he went on to the motorway that it would 'tail' back a kilometre or two because of the notoriously heavy traffic on it!

Certain people proclaim that 'We Are The People' but I chuckled to myself when I thought that when Gulliver first entered Lilliput he must have thought to himself that 'wee are the people' here too, but given that they have agreed to a shared future of equality, they would find themselves 'tied down' to going into negotiations with people whom they have differences of opinion with for the foreseeable future!

It always makes me laugh when I see the name Gibbons as it is an anagram of 'big snob' which is what an old boss of mine was . . . . however people say if you pay peanuts you get monkeys but I got paid peanuts and I wasn't exactly a chimpanzee swinging around on bars in a cage . . . . and if that's not bad enough in return for being paid peanuts I got repeated harassment and non-work-related abuse also!

I was in a bar once before an All Ireland championship game but couldn't figure out if the people around me were referring to the drink or the entertainment as sometimes they were saying the 'decider' would be absorbing stuff but the stuff they were absorbing was 'de cider' also which motivated me to make them the 'butt' of this joke!

When I was in school back during the Eighties I learned that a certain individual was 'excommunicated' from the church . . . . now a few years later there was an injustice being done against me and my 'ex communicated' some sort of an untruth to her friends about me also . . . . however because I was so hurt I wasn't too concerned about 'disfellowship' from a religious organisation at this point but trust me 'this fellow' was rather confused as I have always been so respectful towards everybody!

There is a book called 'Taste Of Bitter Love' . . . . now that reminds me of when I met this northern English lass in a bar here in Dublin one time who asked me 'do you like the taste of bitter love?' to which I replied 'the only 'bitter' I've ever tasted is when I smooched a female Evertonian who'd been sipping lemon juice'!

While listening to a radio station here in Ireland one day they reviewed a film called 'Weather With You' . . . . I laughed to myself that I thought their colleague 'Hugh' fronted the sports bulletins myself and it was the likes of The Met Office who informed us if it would be piddling or not the next day!

Most people are aware of the fact that Israeli people speak Hebrew . . . . now when individuals are in the pub sipping stout and talking to the owner about who made the drink, nearly all are in knowledge of the reality that 'he brew' the beverage alright . . . . but I bet few probably know that Arthur's Day is around the same time as The Day Of Atonement . . . . and it should be even more important to people that they repent as their sins are much more serious 'black stuff'!

A reporter on a news bulletin once remarked that a certain individual had 'landed himself in hot water' . . . . I poked some fun at myself by reflecting that because I suffer from schizophrenia I used to wet the bed as a child and on many occasions I woke up in hot water also but, while the politician may have found himself being hard boiled by opponents, my two eggs in a hanky probably came to close to cracking up like me such was the frustration!

A few years back there was a programme on television where they were obviously trying to provoke hilarity by showing people 'tossing dwarfs' . . . . I thought that if Happy, Dopey, Doc etc . . . were to drop their bags and play with themselves they would be 'tossing dwarfs' also but figured that if someone was to place a 'Mirror Mirror On The Wall' these midgets might see how embarrassing they look from the outside and discontinue doing so!

There was a 2011 Rugby World Cup game where Ireland took on Russia and, on being awarded a scrum, the commentator said 'the Russians have got the 'put in'' . . . . I laughed to my lady friend that I used to have a penfriend in the eastern European country who used to write letters that he would 'put in' the letterbox also . . . . however he was called Boris 'Putin' that is . . . . but while that nation is an old 'socialist' republic the rugby union fraternity would have a very strong right-wing conservative history . . . . and I concluded that it is supposedly wrong to mix sport and politics which is all that he used to converse about!

There's a hurley manufacturer here in Ireland called 'Crooked Stick' . . . . I thought that if Pinocchio was to catch his mickey in his zip after embezelling his boss you'd have a 'crooked stick' also but while he may have been taking the p*ss in both circumstances it could be deemed that his manhood as well as his attitude were a little warped too I'm sure you'll agree!

I was making a cup of coffee one day when I picked up the jar holding the granules and a sticker on it read 'The Rich Short One' . . . . I chuckled to myself that because a local millionaire dwarf wasn't wanting for a few bob he was a 'rich short one' also and figured that if you were to drink too much of the beverage Waterloo wouldn't only be his local train station but would also what you'd be passing lots of in the toilet in addition!

I used to play football with a bloke here in Dublin called Ally Love .... one day I joshed with him that if he was to have sex down a lane-way that would be 'alley love' also but, while he may have been dropped from the starting XI if our manager was to catch him in the act the night before a game, he had similarly dropped his bags and his lady her knickers so they could have some jiggy jiggy in public, ey?!

There's a girl who lives near to me called Melanie Baps who is a really good hockey player .... I laughed to myself that because a survey revealed that Scouse ladies had the largest boobs in the U.K. a while back, there'd be plenty of pairs of 'melony baps in The 'Pool' also alright .... but while some famous sons of Liverpool were Gerry & The Pacemakers, these females are more like 'heart-racers' themselves they're so exciting!

Just prior to an important soccer fixture here in Dublin a while back a sports reporter said 'The Big Two meet tonight' .... I laughed to myself as I thought of a girl that lived close to me in the Raheny area on the north side of the city called Louise who must have had a GG bra cup whom I referred to as being 'big Lou with the big two' also .... and when you think about it her boyfriend and well as the football rivals would regard what they encounter as being a bit of a handful alright!

A while back it was reported on the news that a company 'had gone to the wall' after encountering financial difficulties .... now I reflected upon the fact that back in my early twenties I 'had gone to the wall' on several occasions also .... but it was in a lane way on my way home from the boozer so I could un-zip my jeans and have a p*ss up against it that is .... at least it was only the pints I drank that went into 'liquidation' then though as opposed to the firm who had been employing me, right?!

It always makes me laugh when I listen to my mates favourite album called 'Sock It To Me Biscuits' as if they were to have named the recording 'Sock It To Me Cream Crackers' by mistake it wouldn't be long before some guy called Francie Furey climbed on to the stage wearing boxing gloves and see to it the lead singer was knocked into tomorrow!

ACKNOWLEDGEMENTS

Without trying to sound like a dictator I'm not a great believer in democracy because I believe it is rule by the masses but, although I acknowledge it's what the majority wish for, we haven't half voted in people who have got us into all sorts of debt, ey? . . . . I mean, if they continue to mis-manage, our economy will be about as useful as a blind-folded, one-armed sniper with Parkinson's disease in a 'shoot-the-person-implementing-austerity-measures-at-a-Christmas-party-for-under-privileged-children-which-has-been-gate-crashed-by-incompetent-bankers-trying-to-steal-all-the-toys-Santa-Claus-delivered-to-them' competition!